SONGS FOR A DAUGHTER

*

Peter Ualrig Kennedy

Songs for a Daughter

© Peter Ualrig Kennedy

First Edition 2021

Peter Kennedy has asserted his authorship and given his permission to Dempsey & Windle for these poems to be published here.

Published by Dempsey & Windle under their VOLE imprint

15 Rosetrees
Guildford
Surrey
GU1 2HS
UK
01483 571164
dempseyandwindle.com

British Library Cataloguing-in-Publication Data

A catalogue record for this book is available from the British Library

ISBN: 978-1-913329-46-4

Printed and bound in the UK

for Megan and her carers

Acknowledgements

'Paradelle of a Thousand Ships': published (online) in *London Grip New Poetry*, Autumn 2014

'Sunday morning': published (online) in *Ground*, July 2016

'Three Skeins': unpublished. Highly Commended *(Judge: Carol Ann Duffy)* in Lumen/Camden Poetry Competition 2012

Introduction

In writing poetry about a great hurt, there is a danger of sliding into saccharine sentimentality. The poems collected in this volume are, by their very nature, intensely personal, but I hope that I have avoided that trap. The poems are all about Megan Lucille, the third of our four children, who is learning disabled and is a wheelchair user. She has grown into a beautiful person, although 'lacking capacity', and is loved by our family and by all who meet her. It is true to say that we have had boundless help with the care of our daughter, including at the time of that momentous decision to allow her into residential care. But counselling was scarce in those days; we have had to make our own individual adjustments to our circumstances. Nevertheless, we owe a great debt of gratitude to all of Megan's carers; they are wonderful people.

Megan is a Welsh name meaning "pearl". Lucille is a name of French origin meaning "light".

Megan Lucille – our pearl, our light.

SONGS FOR A DAUGHTER

So it was

at the moment of her birth
the stars trembled in their moorings
constellations shrank to nothing
soon there were silent landslides
the earth opened itself
our feet stumbled on shifting rock

at ten years the deserts crept in
and sandstorms swallowed us
that she could hold a cup was an achievement

so the years proceeded
outstripping her
in her slow progress through life

The day we were told

We were young, your Mum and I, we were untried
    in all the blows that life can give.
We could not see those things that might lie ahead –
    but then, who can?

The paediatrician was sympathetic but direct.
    Your daughter will not develop.
She will be handicapped; maybe she will walk,
    but maybe not.

Anoxic brain damage at your birth
    had stripped you of your capabilities
and of your right to normal life.
    But then, what is normal?

We were sad, we cried, on that dark day,
    but since then you have surpassed so many others
in beauty, in happiness, in spirit.
    You are a child of the light.

Coming back

We went north.
There were portents;
flocks of geese passed overhead,
herons settled in the tops of pine trees.
It was so cold,
and you were not well.

We came back home.
You were dwindling fast, and we rushed
you to hospital in our car;
on the way we thought we had lost you.
The medical team were superb;
they brought you back from that brink.

They managed to get up a drip
to pump fluid into your collapsing circulation;
the cut-downs at each ankle have left their scars,
and when it is cold your feet go blue.
But you have survived these many years now,
and you can live your life.

A little life

What is this, our little life together,
these Sunday afternoons we try not to miss?
On good days we walk along the quayside,
as I push your wheelchair.

Your Mum and I will look out at the river,
at the sparkling water as it flows,
we take pleasure in watching the wading birds
and we keep an eye open for the elusive seal.

We might say 'look, there are some geese …'
knowing that it would mean nothing to you,
we'd have a cheerful one-sided conversation,
hoping for some slight communication.

On cold winter days we'll be content
to have a companionable trip to a garden centre.
We shall walk among the potted plants and say
'see, do you like the pretty flowers …'

In the café you'll enjoy
a cup of tea and a toasted teacake,
or lemon drizzle cake as an extra treat.
And this is our little *precious* life together.

Voiceless

Vocal, nonverbal,
she grew regardless,
hobbledehoy in callipers.
Learnt to hold a fork
and a spoon,
well enough to eat her food.

At last the callipers went.
She rolled her wheelchair around,
pushing at the hand rim.
A battery-driven chair
would have been
well beyond her capabilities.

Vocal, but wordless,
she grew anyhow.
For Christmas at the hospital
I was Santa Claus.
She would come with me
to the Christmas Day ward visit.

There was room for her
to wheel herself
from one bed to another.
The patients loved Santa's little helper,
even when she'd make a beeline
for their grapes.

Every new child arrives in the world contemplating a whole horizon of possibilities

We have come to an ancient church
and I wheel her into the nave
the stained-glass windows mean nothing to her
but she sees the huge overarching space;
her eyes are wide as saucers
it is good to see her response.

We visit an aquarium;
the brightly coloured fish
do not catch her interest;
she speaks no words, she has no language;
she is unable to dress herself;
she cannot cut up her food.

She holds her musical toys to her ear;
if I pick up a guitar she will push my hand towards the strings;
if I sit her at a piano she will guide my hands to the keyboard
in order that I might play for her;
if I show her a mouth organ she will grasp my wrist
she will push my hand up towards my mouth.

She will make the harmonica move from side to side
while I blow random glissandos for her;
if I whisper *let's play Round and Round the Garden*
she will take her time before deciding,
then she will stretch out a hand palm upwards
so that I can walk my fingers round her palm.

It is an achievement.

Her cup

My daughter has a cup
    with her name on.
She can lift it to her lips
    while it is still full
and she can put it down
    when it is empty.

At times when she was away
    for a period of respite care
her cup remained in the kitchen
    waiting for her return
and it seemed to me an act of solidarity
    to drink from her cup.

My bonny girl

my bonny girl who never walked
    I see her walking now
with blossom petals in her hair
all falling from her brow

my pretty girl who'll never dance
    is twirling 'cross the floor
she could dance across the oceans
till she reached the farthest shore

my lovely girl who never spoke
    is speaking in my ear
I understand her every word
though none but I shall hear

those visions come to me at night
    and populate my dreams
when I awake with opened eyes
they vanish like moonbeams

Easter Princess

Once upon a time
you were crowned the Easter Princess
in your little school 'for spastics'.
They did not call it Learning Difficulties then.

You looked so beautiful
in your cardboard crown.
You must have been by then
eight years old, but 'lacking capacity',

Members of the Press
came to photograph the event
for the local paper.
It was a scoop.

You sat there on your small throne,
with your Easter entourage,
looking out at the world.
Wondering what it was all about.

Almost anyone can flourish

The day came when we knew
we were going to have to
let go.

Occasional respite care
would become
long-term residential care.

We weren't going to be taking you
to your little special school
any more.

It was hard.
I had to tell the head teacher
at your little special school

that we wouldn't be bringing you
to school each morning
any more.

Possibly I had not wept
in front of an adult before.
But she was so kind.

She said it would be an opportunity
for you to develop
and to learn new skills.

Almost anyone can flourish
was what she said …
and it's true.

The language of her eyes

Her wonderful carer says
'Megan use your fork' —
left-handed Megan
drops the wedge
of Yorkshire pudding
from her fingers,
lifts her fork,
spears a potato.

I am coming to her residence
where she sits in her wheelchair;
her eyes light up
and I say let us go out
for a walk in the garden
and for tea and cake
by the river.

She speaks no tongue.
In all these many years
no recognisable word
has come from her lips;
but I am sure she knows.
She speaks no words
but I can read
the language of her eyes.

Light in your eyes

I help you out of the car
swivel you round
lift up your palsied feet
place them on the ground

The old routine
the happy cries
you know I am here
there is light in your eyes

Hold me tight

hold me tight my girl
   hug me
   do not let go
as I swing you up from your wheelchair
   and turn you so
to set you down in the car's front seat

where shall we go
   my bonny lass
   to the park
or shall we hit the high road
   hasten to the tall mountains
leave the wheelchair behind

we shall run through the grass
   among the wild daisies
   soar with the birds
fly with the white clouds
   glide through the arc of the rainbow
we will be happy

Able

Able to push her arms into her sleeves
    she grins as I try to get her
    into her parka jacket

Able to push and settle herself snugly
    back into her seat and she laughs
    as I set her down onto her wheelchair

Able to lift a cup to her lips and sip
    then to put it down without spilling
    so long as there is a table top in front of her

Able to push the buttons on her musical toy
    and to make exciting sounds
    through random pressings

Able to guide my hand to the piano keys
    or to the strings of the guitar
    that she cannot play herself

Able to do such wonderful things
    Unable to talk
    Unable to walk

Able to love

Beauty

Beauty is an aurora,
   it is malachite, alchemy,
   it is obsidian, viridian,
it is cornelian.

Beauty is chalcedony,
   it is phosphorescence,
   it is an equinox, it is an alembic,
it is a filament.

Beauty is an escarpment,
   it is an upland meadow,
   it is grass, it is fire,
it is green, it is velvet.

Beauty is alabaster, absinthe,
   amethyst, cerulean,
   Schiehallion, vermilion,
it is amber and pearls.

Beauty is hazel and blue
   in her eyes.
   Such beauty.
It is a blessing.

Dream world

the café on the mezzanine floor
of the shopping mall
    looks out on a dream world
a void which is
    within reach of your gaze
and you seem to see
the afternoon shoppers

who flicker along the aisles
they float up the moving slope
    where you floated too
in your wheelchair
    while I followed and
kept you safe
what can those shoppers

mean to you my girl
here in the café with us
    and at the table we give you
forkful
    after forkful
of Victoria sponge
cake to eat

it is a small joy

Home sweet home

I sit with my first coffee of the day
my map spread out to plan a country walk
where the sere grasses are tall in the pastures
the saltings drowse
by the glittering creek that slides
from the mill

my thought shifts to that other quiet place
where you live with your companions
each with your own room
each as vulnerable as you
your carers are your extended family
I can see on the map the home that is yours

and I can see on the map that you are safe

Magic Sunday

In her dim world in which it seems there is no consciousness of the passage of time or of the nature and indeed existence of Sunday it is on that day once a week that she experiences the pleasure of an afternoon with her Mum and Dad and although she does not know the absolute meaning of routine it is just such a routine with which she has become familiar and in that little life which appears to outside eyes to be devoid of any understanding of language it is the words that are spoken to her by the care staff on those magic Sundays that spark her interest and that nudge the slow gears of her indistinct memory 'Daddy is on his way' and so she sits impassively in her wheelchair intently watching the entry to the residence with the hint of a smile to wait for the twenty or thirty minutes until her Dad rings the doorbell to come in and then a proper grin slowly lights up her pretty face and her carers say that she has without any doubt been waiting for her Dad to arrive which means to her doting and wondering father that there is a lot more going on inside her head than one might realise and he stoops to cradle her shoulders in his arms prior to wheeling her out into the open air and to the waiting car and she laughs aloud in her excitement for she is on the way home.

Sunday morning

Outside, the car doors
thump themselves closed.
   People are leaving church
hurrying through the rain
   to the sanctuary of their motors.
We sit at home
   with the Sunday papers
   and coffee
and our mute daughter.

I lift a square of toast for her.
Steer it to her sparrow mouth,
place it on her tongue.
   A sacrament.

A Sunday visit

Sunday morning, and it's my on call weekend –
let us go up to the hospital.
We shall visit the medical ward
and we'll meet the patients
together.

I know that they like to see you,
the pretty young girl in the wheelchair;
you give each patient one of your big smiles,
and they will chat to you even though you make
no reply.

I am proud of you and your charm;
also I want the patients to see
that the consultant is not a figure on a pedestal,
but a man with his own humanity
and problems.

Once someone put it to me that
this is an ego trip: *See my wounds* …
but I refute that, and I have just noticed
you wheeling yourself to a patient's bedside
and pinching his grapes.

Sunday sonnet

We sit together by the garden wall,
you with your sideways look and secret smile;
'And did you like the apple juice at all?' –
without reply you bend your head awhile.
You pull your nails across the table's top
as if to leave some little scratches there,
but concentration finds a sudden stop,
as you lean backwards in your wheelchair
remaining silent as you always do.
I cannot read the language of your eyes
and soon it's time to go – that's nothing new –
but still I find it hard to realise.
In dreams you often speak to me, and yet
those dreams are ever tempered with regret.

What is it that you see?

You look around you with such intent –
what is it that you see?
We know you cannot speak in words,
we cannot tell how much you understand.

What is it that you see?
You have no spoken language,
but you look around you with such intent –
what is it that you see?

In the car we pass a pillar box,
sturdy and red; and then we glimpse
shining water between the trees.
What is it that you see?

What things exist for you
inside your silent self?
What does the world show to you?
What is it that you see?

Toy box

Inching across the floor you reach
to grasp hold of the toy box,
the low wooden chest with the lid

made long ago by your mama
in the carpentry course that she did
the year that you were born.

Decades pass, each by each,
and life deals in hard knocks,
but you are a determined kid;

inching across the floor you reach
the low wooden chest with the lid.
You know just where the toys are hid.

Avatar

Hearing them arrive,
I filled the bath with water
and added a large packet of salt.

They wheeled her into the bathroom –
she's part octopus, part luminescence
they said, carefully lowering her in.

I bent over the bath to feel her smooth mottled skin,
and she uncoiled two of her tentacles,
raising them up to my face,

and as she gently touched my cheek
she glowed all over
with a fiery brightness.

The radiance lasted well into the evening
as I sat reading in the sanctified glow
of her octopus luminescence.

Having a bath

She likes having a bath –
she can splash about,
and she can do that trick with her wet soapy hands,
squeezing her palms together
to make the sound of a raspberry,
which makes her squeal with laughter.

They have a hoist where she lives now
which is something we lacked
when she was still with us,
but she was younger and lighter then,
and we were able to lift her out,
even when she was all soapy.

The hoist, then, is the added ingredient,
the piece of kit that makes it possible
to bath this adult child
who is unable to stand unaided.
That was what we lacked.
It would have made all the difference.

The girl who found the lost chord

Out of the corner of her eye she spies the piano
that digital upright
which sits by the wall
with all the quality and power
of a concert grand.

She wheels herself
across the room until she can reach
the keyboard and press the keys
in their clumps
and tinkle small random notes

when of a sudden,
with a chance nudge of her elbow,
she has hit the sustain button
and a huge resounding chord
swells into her hearing.

As the chord pulses and hangs,
her eyes have rounded
with amazement.
She hears the sound of the angels
and the angels sing to her.

In fine voice

You are in fine voice today
calling out your joy to the sun
with wordless elation at being free,
out of doors,
     going somewhere new.

The rainbow has turned itself over,
a many-coloured upside-down cake
with its feet in the sky,
its harlequin spine curled and
     nestled in the hills.

The rainbow has its paws in the air,
it lies on its back waiting to be tickled,
as you stretch out your hand
palm up so that we can play
     'Round and Round the Garden'.

A fine young lady in fine voice
with me trundling your wheelchair
we make a fine team
on such a fine day.
     You coulda been a contender.

Thank you

We walk in bright sunshine
along the river path.
A young man comes towards us –
slim and neat;
Eastern European, my guess.

He sees our daughter's strabismus gaze,
stops beside her wheelchair.
He inclines his head
and speaks quietly to her
– thank you – he says to our daughter.

Her face is illumined by the summer sun
and she smiles,
but having no words
and little comprehension
she does not reply.

The young man again says
– thank you –
he bends forward,
he lifts her hand to his lips
and he kisses the back of her hand.

Letting her hand drop
he says once more to her
– thank you –
and he smiles at us
before resuming his walk.

I can think of nothing to say to him
save for a weak *take care*
and so we walk on
slowly
as I push the wheelchair.

But for some moments
my eyes are
misty
with foolish
tears.

She was dancing

I dreamed last night
    that she was dancing,
wheelchair abandoned where it stayed;
the ballroom walls
    were broken and decayed;
dust in the air picked out
each glancing
    flash of light
as the glitter ball swayed.
    And she was dancing.

Basement of dreams

in the basement of dreams
in its gloomy obscurity
he picks his dubious way
over rubble

fungi protrude
from dank walls
there are dirt specks on
a cobwebbed door

push through
to where no people are
in the glittering ballroom
full of voices

a straw haired cloth doll sprawls
on a gilded chair
he lifts her in his arms
they dance on the tilting floor

he is oppressed
unable to breathe
the weight on his chest
is insupportable

turn him carefully
say the voices
and a hundred hands
deliver him to the light

At home in exile

At home in exile there is little to hold me
close to the world we once lived in

now existence is virtual
but the books and the poetry

lift my laggard soul to the heavens
and when I dream

I dream of mansions of stone and marble
I swim in gilded pools

and I dream of you dancing
laughing

in the place where you live
in your house of gold

it must be of gold if you are there
and I am in exile at home

Days of separation

In those days of separation
we could not visit you
could not see you
could not embrace you
could not hold you
could not speak the words to you
    that were in our hearts.

After months the moment came
when we could see you
when they brought you by car
so that we might talk
through the open window
but we could not come near
    we could not hold you.

You smiled and looked happy
although you could not understand
but we knew that you were well
we knew that you were cared for
we knew that you were safe
it was enough
    it was all that we had.

Laces

It's ten to midnight
as I unlace my shoes.
My girl,
you will never have
that satisfaction
that ease
of tying
or of untying
your shoelaces.

Ten to midnight,
seven in the morning –
time has no meaning.

Nor do shoelaces.

Mosaic

Without you we'd be diminished –
you are part of the mosaic of our family life.
Families grow, mature, split up;
the mosaic fragments,

each daughter and son go on their adult ways,
they forge new lives, but you –
you float in your haze-dimmed world
as in a waking dream.

On Christmas Day things change,
we come together,
our cheer and chatter fill the hours,
and it is a delight to you.

Skittles

let's go tenpin bowling
    I said
and you smiled
you looked happy

you had heard my words
    of course
but you could not have understood
I don't think you understand words

I don't think you get the meanings
    although
you can feel the mood
and you are happy

we trundle to the bowling alley
    where I set up
the chute on which to balance
the heavy bowling ball

the bowling ball teeters on the chute
    while I position
your wheelchair a good six feet behind
the bowling chute

you can see the ball balancing
    and without words
you know what you want to do
there is an image in your mind

so without hesitating you wheel yourself
    forward
and stretch out your hand
to prod the bowling ball

away it rolls and you are pleased
    it does not matter
where the ball has gone
the skittles are not a consideration

you have done something important
    and you are happy
you have pushed that ball away
and you are happy

Star

Though your eyes may be clouded and your vision dim,
in those eyes I see joy and laughter twinkling
then at times when you seem pensive
I believe your hobbled mind is thinking
with particular intent.

As on the day you had your mini-disco
in the summerhouse at your home
where you were holding a string of fairy lights
that glittered brightly in the gloaming,
and you wondered what they meant.

Fingering the lights in that little hut
there were questions behind your eyes –
whatever were those bright stars that you held?
Stars newly fallen from the skies,
holding an intelligence unspent.

Stars that had surged into that meagre shed,
to take their place within your questing gaze –
was there some way that they might light a spark,
and set your dormant mind ablaze,
by some strange happy accident?

I know in my heart this could never be.
You are loved so much for what you are;
loved for your beauty and for your trust,
our true and shining star.
And for this we must remain content.

Mount Rushmore

Wrapped in the silence of your mind
    you look at the world through the car window
while I dream that Freddie Mercury
    has been added to Mount Rushmore.

Today it is our Sunday drive, my girl,
    and in your life you have never spoken.
You seem to register what you see;
    I cannot tell what you are thinking.

The café where they are always kind
    is a good place for us to stop.
They will make a space for your wheelchair,
    we shall have lemon cake and fizzy drink.

You look around wide-eyed,
    above us a ceiling fan is whirring.
It catches your eye. You have never spoken.
    Now of a sudden you say fan distinctly.

This is a waking dream in which I am entwined;
    when I truly wake you won't be talking
and the face of Freddie Mercury
    won't be on Mount Rushmore.

Making sense of it all

Some avenging angel wearing a black fedora
swooped down from Heaven's vault
and nipped off with our daughter's
    newly-minted mind and soul.

Up in Heaven they began to play with them,
the angels hoofed her soul about a bit,
they prodded it rather roughly,
    to see how far it would roll.

They decided it needed painting.
Carmine red was what they'd use –
but God, on hearing the commotion, said
    White, only white, for her soul!

White would be for innocence,
she would never know malice or hate;
so the angels did what God told them,
    with the whitest paint they could find.

Then the angel with the black fedora
brought the beautiful soul back to earth,
and our daughter has always been lovely –
    but they forgot to bring back her mind.

That's what it's all about

Sometimes when I lie awake
I think of what you might have been –

you might have been a dancer,
or a girl who played the tambourine.

You might have been a barrister,
a doctor, or a nurse,

or a typist or a journalist,
or the Keeper of the Purse.

On that day they told your Mum and Dad
that you would never walk

you had no words to contradict,
and you have never learned to talk.

It doesn't matter any more –
you will never be without

our fervent and undying love.
That's what it's all about.

The tablet

And this has been your Christmas present,
a simple tablet.
Not a tablet of stone
but a tablet of Fire,
of strange depths and puzzlement.

You can look through its window
as if looking deep into a mirror,
and – if we can master the technology –
you will be able to see us there
and we shall be able to see you.

We shall be able to speak to you.
Hello, hello, can you hear us?
You are looking so happy today ...
You do not answer –
so we shan't know
if it means anything to you.

No matter –
we can see you smiling
and laughing as you grab the screen
and press it to your ear;
the screen goes dark
but you can hear our chatter.

In this way we stay in touch
in these difficult times.
Each time we call
we see that you are happy
and safe.
It means so much.

We were dancing

One brave afternoon we took you to the tea dance –
a special occasion in the village hall,
for a young woman with cerebral palsy.

It was her self-imposed challenge
to walk one circuit of the hall
unaided. So she did it.

She did it and everyone applauded;
the small band played
For She's a Jolly Good Fellow –

No bowing to feminist sensibilities there.
When they started to play a waltz,
you and I took to the floor.

I twirled you round in your wheelchair
to the rhythm of the music,
and you were ecstatic.

The young woman with walking difficulties
came over in her own wheelchair
and gave you a companionable hug.

When the next tune started I helped you to stand,
and for a few bright moments
we were dancing.

A dream of flight

from her window she sees
 the curved flight of the swift –
a freedom of gulls
 makes her heart lift

a butterfly flitters past
 sidestepping motes of dust
she slides onto her wheelchair
 needs must

push the hand rims and roll
 towards the open air
to the tree lined street
 to the sun-struck square

the wheels take her on
 her line of flight
and on the frame – a logo:
 '*Freedom Lite*'

You are no changeling

You are no changeling, sweetheart,
you are our darling one,
you are our sweet girl
with no thought beyond your music box,
your yellow plastic phone with all the tunes,
the toy you play with most when you're at home.

Sprat

thou little sprat
thou chickadee
thou bobbing wren
thou vivid spark
thou sweet girl

thou child

In that vast city

In that vast city of my dreams
I find the daughter who I thought was lost

I clamber up the never-ending steps
and she is there, a smiling laughing girl

we dance, we sing, she is as light as air,
she has no need of crutches, has no wheelchair

A splinter of ice has entered my heart
a sliver of silver has pierced my tongue.

Why did you go, you silly tart,
so young. So young.

silly from sælig (Old English): blessed.
tart (Australian slang): a girl or woman, implying admiration.

Three skeins

Three skeins of geese
  so high, so high.
Three kisses for you
  and one sigh.

Three kisses for love,
  one sigh for grief.
The geese pass above.
  Time is a thief.

The skeins have flown by;
  gone are the geese.
You are with me
  for too short a lease.

Shirt

My shirt sails across the room
arms flailing
   like a wounded bird.
It lands – so – on the chair back.

She couldn't have done that,
I thought,
   my daughter
cannot throw things.

She cannot use a knife and fork,
she cannot speak,
   my wounded girl.
What will she do when I am gone?

She is happy where she is;
she is loved and cared for,
   and of course I know.
She will forget me.

Round and Round the Garden

One day
after these many long months
of separation

we shall see each other
once again
and hug.

Will you remember us?
Will you remember
how to hold out your hand

palm up and
will you remember
how we used to play

Round and Round the Garden?

The day will come

When we are gone
will you remember?
When we are not here,
when we are   not,
what will you recall?

Will there be a gap left,
when we are   not?
Would you remember
if you were to hear
the sound of our voices?

If we were to record our voices
that could be unfair –
for if you were to hear us
you might think
that we were still here.

The day will come
when we are   not,
and you will not recall us;
but your brother and your sisters
will remember for you.

The day will come
when we are   not,
and you will not recall us.
We pray that you will then be
enfolded in the love of others.

Paradelle of a thousand ships

A family picture shows us gathered on the lawn.
A family picture shows us gathered on the lawn.
Informal. All together. Happy with ourselves.
Informal. All together. Happy with ourselves.
A gathered family shows ourselves together,
Informal picture, happy the lawn with us all on.

I wore pale trousers, white shoes. No grey hair.
I wore pale trousers, white shoes. No grey hair.
My beard was dark then, Helen, and your dark curls.
My beard was dark then, Helen, and your dark curls.
White my trousers and shoes, pale Helen; dark was I,
Dark beard hairs. Your curls wore no grey then.

One palsied daughter in her wheelchair. The others kneel, or stand.
One palsied daughter in her wheelchair. The others kneel, or stand.
A fleet of years set sail that distant day.
A fleet of years set sail that distant day.
Stand, distant daughter, fleet the palsied wheelchair years --
That, or kneel; sail her one day in a set of others.

Stand, others; picture trousers, curls, white lawn, dark family;
Hair was wore informal. A set of ourselves
Shows us the palsied day -- or a dark wheelchair;
And then the years that fleet on, all distant.
Sail, happy Helen, one with your daughter together gathered;
I, in my shoes, grey beard, kneel, pale. No her.